AN EXPEDITION TOWARD A DEEPER RELATIONSHIP WITH GOD

LEADER GUIDE
BETH MOORE
WITH KATHY STRAWN
LIFEWAY PRESS®
NASHVILLE, TN

Requests for permission should be addressed in writing to
LifeWay Press®
One LifeWay Plaza
Nashville, TN 37234-0172

ISBN 9781535909600
Item 005804823

Dewey Decimal Classification Number: 268.432
Subject Heading: Discipleship—Curricula\God\Bible—Study
Dewey Decimal Classification Number: 248.82
Subject Heading: CHRISTIAN LIFE \ JESUS CHRIST—TEACHINGS

Printed in the United States of America
LifeWay Kids
LifeWay Resources
One LifeWay Plaza
Nashville, Tennessee 37234-0172

We believe the Bible has God for its author; salvation for its end; and truth, without any mixture of error, for its matter and that all Scripture is totally true and trustworthy. To review LifeWay's doctrinal guideline, please visit *lifeway.com/doctrinalguideline.*



# About the Authors

**Beth Moore** is a best-selling book and Bible study author and a dynamic teacher whose conferences take her across the globe. Beth lives in Houston, Texas, where she leads Living Proof Ministries with the purpose of encouraging and teaching women to know and love Jesus through the study of Scripture.

Beth and her husband, Keith, have two adult daughters and three delightful grandchildren. They are devoted to the local church and have the privilege of attending Bayou City Fellowship in Houston, Texas.

Beth's life is full of activity, but one commitment remains constant: counting all things but loss for the excellence of knowing Christ Jesus, the Lord (Phil. 3:8).

**Kathy Strawn** has been writing kids' curriculum for LifeWay Kids for over 30 years, including kids' versions of the Beth Moore Bible studies: *Jesus the One and Only* and *Beloved Disciple* and Priscilla Shirer's *Unseen: The Armor of God for Kids*. She has taught Sunday School and discipleship classes for children for many years at First Baptist Church, College Station, Texas, and now assists her husband in their Ministry of Education by consulting with churches about their children's programs.

# Table of Contents

# The Quest

## GROWING CLOSER TO GOD IS OUR QUEST

*Through this study children can...*

**DISCOVER**
that there is no one like God and He wants to interact with His creation, especially people.

**UNDERSTAND**
how sin distorts our relationship with God, but that God made a plan to restore us to Him.

**REALIZE**
the importance of questions in growing closer to God.

*Key Verse:*

"Ask, and it will be given to you. Seek, and you will find. Knock, and the door will be opened to you."
Matthew 7:7

# EMBARK

**YOU WILL NEED:**

- ☐ "Administration Guide and Question Words" (Item 1)

**TO DO:**

- ☐ Post each question word in a different area of the room.

**TEACHING TIP**

If you teach a small group of kids, give each kid two craft sticks on which he can write his name. While the Questioner is counting, the other kids drop their sticks near two different question words. When the Questioner names his question word, any kid who has a stick near that word, picks it up to put in a pile in the middle. Play continues until only one stick is left. The student whose name is on that stick is the winner.

## MEET THE QUESTIONER

➤ Welcome kids as they arrive.

➤ Call attention to the question words in the different areas of the room. Invite a volunteer to be the "Questioner" and to stand in the middle of the room. Mention that the Questioner will cover and close his eyes, count to ten, and call out one of the question words before opening his eyes. Explain that while the Questioner is counting, other kids will move to stand near a question word. When the Questioner calls his question word, any kids at that word will move to the center of the room and will count with the Questioner the next time he counts to ten. Play continues until only one kid is left. That kid becomes the new Questioner and all kids join the game for another round of play.

➤ Ask kids, "What are some questions that you ask every day? What are some questions you ask your parents? Teachers? Coaches? Church leaders? Pastor?"

➤ Mention that questions are an important part of this study and will help kids move further along in their adventure with God. Ask kids to share questions they already have about what will happen during their time in the study. Expect questions such as "Will we have snacks?"

# EXPLORE

**YOU WILL NEED:**

- ☐ "Five Questions" (Item 2)
- ☐ "God Is ..." (Item 3)
- ☐ "My Prayer" (Item 4)
- ☐ "Matthew 7:7 Poster" (Item 7)
- ☐ Activity Books
- ☐ Two large sheets of paper
- ☐ Marker
- ☐ Pencils

**TO DO:**

- ☐ Print the words of Matthew 7:7 on one large paper.
- ☐ Print "My Prayer" for each kid you expect.

### 1. INTRODUCE THE QUEST

- ➤ Point out that when we think of quests, we think of brave adventures. Explain that a quest is a journey to find something. Ask: "Have you ever been on an adventure?"
- ➤ Say: "In our study, we will go on a quest to find answers to questions that will help us grow closer to God. We will have an adventure in God's Word, the Bible. The Bible is our instruction book on how to know God and how to live for Him. God wants us to go on an adventure with Him and grow closer to Him as we explore each day."
- ➤ Slowly draw a question mark on a large sheet of paper as kids guess what you are drawing. Note for the kids that the word quest is part of the word question. Ask whether kids think having a conversation without asking any questions would be easy or hard.
- ➤ Pair the kids. *(Be part of a pair yourself if needed.)* Instruct the kids to conduct a one-minute conversation with their partners without asking any questions. Time the conversations. Ask whether the task was easy or hard.
- ➤ Mention that in this quest, kids will use 5 main questions (where, who, what, why, how) to help them advance toward the goal of growing closer to God. Remark that the Bible contains many questions — about 3,300 of them! God asks questions of people. People ask questions of God. People ask each other questions.
- ➤ Ask kids why they think God would ask anyone questions when He already knows everything. After their answers, respond that one possible reason is that God, the One who made people, wants people to talk with Him. Note also that God

sometimes asks questions of people so that they will think about the questions, what God is trying to teach them, and how they will respond.

### 2. TELL THE BIBLE STORY

➤ Point out that questions are a big part of today's Bible story. Challenge the kids to draw a question mark in the air with their index fingers whenever they hear a question during the Bible story.

➤ Tell the following Bible story in your own words with your Bible open to Genesis 1–3.

**GOD'S VERY GOOD PLAN / GENESIS 1–3**

*In the beginning, nothing existed except God. God went to work. He spoke and created light. He separated the water on earth from the water above the earth to make the sky.*

*God made the dry land and the seas. He commanded the earth to grow plants and trees. He placed the sun, moon, and stars in the sky.*

*God created all living things in the water and all birds that fly. He added animals to cover the earth. God looked down at His creation and knew that it was good.*

*God created people. He made people special. God created people in His own image. God made a man, Adam, from dust of the ground. He breathed into the man, and the man became alive. God took a rib from the man and created a woman. Adam named his wife Eve.*

*God instructed the man and woman to care for the garden where He had placed them and to take care of the earth. God warned Adam and Eve: "You may eat of any tree in the garden except that you must not eat of the tree of knowledge of good and evil. If you eat of this tree, you will die."*

*The serpent questioned Eve.* (Use her name and give the kids a clue that you are asking the first question). *"Did God really say that you cannot eat of any tree in the garden?" he asked.* (Wait as kids finger-draw their question marks.)

*Eve answered, "We can eat of any tree except the one in the middle of the garden. God told us we would die if we eat it or touch it."*

*Satan lied, "No! You won't die. God just knows that if you eat the fruit, you will be like Him, knowing good and evil."*

*The fruit of the tree looked so good. Eve thought about being as wise as God. She took some of the fruit and ate it.*

*She gave some to Adam to eat. He knew it was wrong to eat the fruit, but he ate it anyway.*

*Suddenly Adam and Eve realized they had no clothes on. They sewed leaves together to cover themselves. That evening, Adam and Eve heard God walking in the garden. They quickly hid themselves. God called to Adam, "Where are you?"* (Wait as kids make their question marks.)

*Adam answered, I heard you in the garden. I was afraid since I have no clothes on. So I hid."*

*God asked, "Who told you that you were naked? Did you eat of the tree I told you not to eat from?"* (Wait for kids to make their question marks.)

*Adam blamed Eve and God. "The woman You made for me gave me fruit and I ate it."*

*When God asked what she had done, Eve blamed the serpent. "The serpent tricked me," she said.*

*God punished the serpent. He punished Eve. He punished Adam. Yet, God also gave Adam and Eve hope. He promised that one day a descendant of Adam and Eve would crush the serpent.*

## 3. MAKE THE CHRIST CONNECTION

➤ Since Adam and Eve, everyone has sinned against God. Our sin separates us from God. God promised that one of Eve's descendants would put an end to sin and death. God sent His Son, Jesus, to live as Adam didn't—perfectly sinless. God the Son came into the world to rescue people from sin and bring them back to God. Jesus came to earth on a quest to rescue you from sin.

## 4. STUDY THE BIBLE

➤ Guide the kids to locate Genesis 3 in their Bibles. Ask: Did God talk to people in the Bible? (*Yes.*)

➤ Call on a volunteer to read verses 8 and 9 aloud. Ask what kids heard God say. (*A question*)

➤ Place the "Where are you?" question before the group. Remind kids that God knows everything, and He knew exactly where Adam and Eve were. Emphasize that God wants people to come to Him and ask for forgiveness of their sins. God came to Adam and Eve so they could recognize their sin and ask for forgiveness.

- Direct the kids to find the question in verse 11 as well as who asked it and to whom it was asked. Place the "Who told you?" question before the group. Point out the difference between God telling a person about something and Satan telling a person about something. Emphasize that Satan always tries to deceive people, and one way people can defeat him is to learn what God says about us, others, our pasts, and our futures. Hold your Bible as you remark that the Bible is God's truth about these things.
- God wanted Adam and Eve to ask for forgiveness. Instead they blamed the serpent and each other for their sin. Sin hurts not only our relationship with God, but also with each other.
- Form small teams and give each one a "God Is …" assignment. Direct teams to find and read their Bible verses and to tell what each one says about God. Call for reports of the teams. Ask: "When God said that He would send a chosen one to defeat the serpent, what was God promising to do?" (*send a Savior, Jesus*) "Why did God send Jesus?" (*to die for us, to save us*) Affirm kids in what they have learned.
- Distribute an Activity Book to each child. Lead kids to complete page 8 as a review of today's study of Genesis 1–3.

### 5. FOCUS ON THE MEMORY VERSE

- Explain to kids that we know God not only sent Jesus on a quest, but that Jesus asked questions. Tell kids to listen to the verse you are going to read about Jesus and to draw a question mark in the air when they hear about Jesus asking questions. Read Luke 2:45-47.
- Ask: "Why do you think Jesus asked questions?" (*pause for answers*) Explain that Jesus was very good at asking questions later as a grown man, too. Jesus asked questions for the same reason God did in the Old Testament. He wanted people to think about the question, what He was trying to teach them, and how they would respond.
- Ask: "Do you think God wanted people to know about His rescue mission?" (*Yes, He told them many times*) "We are going to talk several times about how Jesus loves us and wants us to be forgiven. Let's learn a verse about how Jesus told us to ask questions!"
- Lead the kids to read the display of Matthew 7:7. Explain that these words were spoken by Jesus as He taught His followers. Ask what words in the verse relate to questions. If the kids do not mention knock along with ask and seek, point out that knock refers to asking to enter.

- Suggest that kids use hand motions to help them learn the verse. Possible actions are finger-drawing question marks for ask, shielding eyes like binoculars for seek, and pantomiming knock. Lead the kids to repeat the verse several times using the hand motions.
- Invite kids to turn in their Activity Books to p. 8. Lead them to complete the "Matthew 7:7 Puzzle." Be sure to point out how the beginning letters of ask, seek, and knock spell ASK.

**6. PRAY**

- Distribute "My Prayer" pages. Note for kids that the different spaces are labeled with questions God is asking everyone. They are much like the questions God asked Adam and Eve in Genesis 3. Make sure kids understand what each of the questions is asking of them. Assure kids they will learn more about these questions during other sessions of the study.
- Direct kids to complete these pages and use them as they pray silently to God. Urge the kids to pray, thanking God for sending Jesus as part of His great rescue plan, that He loved us that much, and that He wants us to have a relationship with Him.
- Tell the group that for several minutes, kids will spread out in the room to work in silence answering the questions on the page and talking to God about what they wrote.
- After a few minutes, or when you notice most kids are finished praying, call the group back together and transition to small group activities.

# ENGAGE

- Transition kids into small groups, dividing them into an older group and a younger group. If you have a large group of either older or younger kids, form groups of about 5 or 6 kids. Distribute the Activity Books and pencils. Direct the boys and girls to write their names on the outside front cover.
- Complete "Dig Deeper" in this week's Activity Book together. As time permits, guide kids to complete additional activities until time to begin the application activities.

## ENGAGE ACTIVITY 1: CREATE AND PLAY "I QUESTION"

**YOU WILL NEED:**

- ☐ Sheets of paper (either copy paper or construction paper work well)
- ☐ Markers
- ☐ Large sheet of paper
- ☐ Scissors
- ☐ Number cube

**TO DO:**

- ☐ Create game pieces by printing point numbers (100, 400, 500, etc.) and game instructions such as Move forward 2 spaces or Say Memory Verse for 200 points on separate sheets of paper.

- ➤ Suggest the group make a special pathway game to help them recall facts about the Bible story, the memory verse, and the quest to be close to God.
- ➤ Ask the kids what questions they could ask about today's Bible story using who as the first word. Print kids' responses on a large sheet of paper. Continue with the question word *where* and then other questions kids think of related to today's study. If no one suggests asking how many questions are included in the Bible, suggest it yourself. Then remind kids the Bible has about 3,300 questions.
- ➤ Distribute sheets of paper. If you have fewer than 8 children, give each child two or three sheets to prepare for the game. Guide the boys and girls to make a large question mark on the floor using the sheets of paper, mixing the points and instructions. Allow one kid to cut out a large circle and to print Finish on it. Place the circle at the bottom of the question mark path.
- ➤ Separate the group into two teams. Call on a student to toss the cube and step onto the question mark path to move that many steps. If the student lands on a "points" card and can answer the first question on the large paper, the team is awarded the points. If the student lands on an "instruction card," she must first follow the instructions and then answer a question. If correct, the team is awarded 100 points. When a second player takes a turn, he tosses the cube, changes places with the child on the question mark, and moves forward the number of steps indicated. If a child answers a question incorrectly, play moves to the next kid. Keep playing in this manner until the team reaches the dot at the end of the question mark.
- ➤ If time allows, play the game again, mixing up the papers that make up the pathway.
- ➤ Lead the group to recall the five questions they are learning to use in their quest for growing closer to God.

- Lead the group in prayer, asking God to help kids learn how to have a closer relationship with God as they learn how to ask God questions and to listen to the answers.

## ENGAGE ACTIVITY 2: MAKE AN "INQUIRING MINDS" WALL DISPLAY

**YOU WILL NEED:**

- ☐ "Inquiring Minds Assignments" (Item 5)
- ☐ Tape (painter's tape is especially good for use on walls)
- ☐ Three half-sheets of construction paper
- ☐ Markers

- Explain that the many questions in the Bible (about 3,300) are asked. Most questions are from God to people, people to God, and people to people. Emphasize that God is pleased when people ask Him questions in an effort to know more about Him. Even when people ask God questions that seem to show disbelief, they are continuing their relationship with Him and can come to belief.
- Suggest that kids make a wall display sharing information about several Bible questions. Assist kids in attaching two long vertical lengths of tape to the wall about 2 feet apart. Distribute three half-sheets of construction paper. Ask one person to print on one sheet "Who asked the question?" Another kid can print "What question was asked?" A third student can print "To whom was the question asked?" Place the first question to the left of the left hand length of tape, the second between the tape lines, and the last one to the right of the right hand length of tape. Note for kids that they now have three columns with titles.
- Direct the kids to work in pairs choosing an assignment card, reading the Bible passage, deciding on answers, and attaching the answers to the correct column on the wall. Give guidance as needed, but let kids work on their own as much as possible. Pairs may work on additional assignments as time allows.
- Review the completed wall display with the kids. Remind them that questions can help them grow closer to God. Together name the major questions kids studied during this session. Remind kids they will be studying during the week ahead about these questions and answers in their Activity Books.

# EXAMINE

**YOU WILL NEED:**

- ☐ "Review Questions" (Item 6)
- ☐ Bible
- ☐ Activity Book
- ☐ Two paper plates per kid
- ☐ Two craft sticks per kid
- ☐ Markers

➤ Form a circle. Invite the kids to play "I'm Going on an Adventure." Explain you will start, "I'm going on an adventure, and I'm going to take a compass," and the next person will repeat your statement and add what he will take.

➤ Play continues as each player down the line repeats each previous player's answer and then adds his own.

➤ Remind kids that their quest to grow closer to God is a real-life adventure and also needs equipment. Remark that the only tool people must have for their quest is something that can only be used when it is open. Let kids guess what it is. If no one guesses correctly, add that the item is found in most homes and is both old and new. Emphasize the Bible is the item needed for this quest.

➤ Hold up an Activity Book. Tell kids this book is designed to help them along on their adventure. People must plan time daily to pray and read the Bible.

➤ Suggest the group pray, thanking God for wanting to have a relationship with them. Ask for a volunteer to pray aloud, or pray yourself.

➤ Review this session's Bible story with a game: Give each kid two paper plates and two craft sticks. Assign each kid two numbers (so that you have the numbers from 1 to double the number of kids you have). Let the kid print each number on a different plate and on a different stick. Collect the sticks. Direct the kids to form a large circle with the plates. As you clap your hands, kids will walk around the plates to the right. When you stop clapping, the kids move to stand beside one plate. Choose one number stick. The kid beside that number answers a review question. If no kid is beside the stick called, the entire group repeats Matthew 7:7 together. Play until parents arrive.

➤ As kids leave, remind them to complete this week's Activity Book pages.

# The Quest & Faith

## FOLLOWING GOD'S PLAN

*Purpose: Through this study children can*

**DISCOVER**
Abraham's God-given quest.

**UNDERSTAND**
that God always does what is right and just.

**REALIZE**
that growing closer to God is a quest for a lifetime.

*Key Verse:*

"For everyone who asks receives, and the one who seeks finds, and to the one who knocks, the door will be opened."
Matthew 7:8

# EMBARK

**YOU WILL NEED:**

- ☐ Masking tape or painter's tape

**TO DO:**

- ☐ Make two long tape lines as far apart as possible, up to about 20 feet. Each line should be long enough for all the kids to stand beside each other.

## COME AND GO

- Welcome kids as they arrive.
- Invite the kids to play a game of "Come and Go." Designate one kid to be the caller and to stand behind one tape line. Direct the other kids to line up side by side about two feet in front of the caller – and then to turn their backs on the caller. Kids will be directed by the caller to either come (move toward the caller) or to go (move away from the caller). The caller will give one of the two directions. Kids follow that direction until the caller changes it. The object of the game is to be the first to cross the second tape line. The student who first crosses the line is the caller for the next round. Play several rounds of the game.
- After the game, explain that the directions come and go might seem confusing when used together, but coming and going are exactly what God wants of His followers. In today's session, we are going to discover how believers can be both coming and going.

# EXPLORE

**YOU WILL NEED:**
- ☐ "Matthew 7:7 Poster" (Item 7)
- ☐ "Matthew 7:8 Poster" (Item 8)
- ☐ "Study the Bible Signs" (Item 9)
- ☐ "Fill in the Blank Story" (Item 14)
- ☐ 3-foot length of yarn
- ☐ Three large sheets of paper
- ☐ Marker or pen

**TO DO:**
- ☐ Post both of the Matthew 7 posters, but turn the "Matthew 7:8 Poster" so the back shows.
- ☐ Display the "Study the Bible Signs" on different walls or areas of the room.

### 1. INTRODUCE THE QUEST

➤ Remind the kids that a *quest* is a search for something, and that the quest for this study is the adventure of growing closer to God.

➤ Show the length of yarn. Explain that the yarn represents your quest for growing closer to God, with one end being your birthday and the other the end of your life.

➤ Take hold of the yarn at any place and remark that when a person becomes a Christian, he has taken an important step in his quest of growing closer to God. Explain that sometimes people do not realize that part of their quest happens even before their decision to accept Christ as Savior. Mention that God begins directing people, guiding them, loving them, and calling them to come to Him from the very beginning of their lives. God places people in families, provides for their needs, and shows Himself through creation, the Bible, and people.

➤ Point out that after a person becomes a Christian, the quest continues. Remark that God continues to direct, guide, love, and call people to come to Him, but then He also asks them to go. God wants believers to go with their knowledge of Him to share the news with everyone and to serve others. Note for kids that God calls people to Him and then directs them to go. Mention that believers do not quit asking questions and seeking closeness with God, but continue that all their lives.

➤ Point out that kids are already on this journey of a lifetime. Explain that some in the group may have already accepted Jesus as their Savior and have answered God's call to come to Him. Note for kids that others may be seriously thinking about becoming a Christian but have questions they want to ask. These kids may be ready to talk to someone about their questions. Assure kids that teachers will be glad to talk with anyone who wishes, but that parents, children's ministers, and pastors are also good choices for that conversation. Tell kids that some may be just beginning to ask questions about what becoming a believer involves. Explain that you or the people already named can help them move forward in their quest.

## 2. TELL THE BIBLE STORY

### *ABRAM'S JOURNEY*
### *GENESIS 12:1-3 AND GENESIS 15:1-21*

*Abram lived with his wife, Sarai. One day, God called out to Abram. God had chosen Abram and told him to leave home and move to a place where he had never been. God promised Abram three things: a large family, land for his family, and blessing. Later, God visited Abram in a vision and said, "Do not be afraid, Abram. I am your shield; your reward will be very great."*

*God's promise was good, but Abram was sad because he didn't have any children to inherit his blessing. "One of my slaves will be my heir," Abram cried. But God's plan was boundless. He let Abram outside to remind him of His promise. "Look at the sky and count the stars, if you can," God said. Abram couldn't count the stars. There were too many! "Your family will be that numerous," God promised. Abram believed God, and God was pleased.*

*God also promised that Abram's family would keep the land they were living in. Abram asked, "How can I be sure?" So God confirmed His covenant with Abram.*

*God told Abram to bring five animals: a cow, a goat, a ram, a turtledove, and a pigeon. Abram did as God said, and he divided the animals. Then, when the sun was setting, a deep sleep came over him.*

*While Abram slept, God told him what would happen in the future. He said that Abram's family would be slaves in another country for 400 years. After these 400 years, God would judge the nation and bless Abram's family. And God promised that in spite of all the difficult things would happen, Abram would live a long and peaceful life.*

*After sunset, once it was dark, a smoking pot of fire and a flaming torch representing God passed between the divided animals. This sign demonstrated that God would be responsible for keeping His promise.*

### 3. MAKE THE CHRIST CONNECTION

- God called Abram to leave his country and family to go to another land. God promised to bless all the world through Abram. God sent Jesus from His home in heaven to be born on earth into Abram family. Through Jesus, all the nations of the earth are blessed.
- Point out to the kids that God promised children to Abram, but that God gave Abram even more than he asked. Explain that Abram was the ancestor to more people than the stars in the sky or grains of sand on the beach. (Gen. 22:17) Recall with the group that one of the questions discussed during the last meeting was "How much more?" Remark that God kept the promise with the birth of Isaac, but God blessed Abram with "so much more" because one of Abram descendants was Jesus, the Savior of the world!
- Guide kids to locate Romans 5:6-11, asking them to notice the phrase *how much more* (v. 9). Explain that Jesus gives so much more than just being saved from sin. Point out that Jesus gives believers His presence, His love, and His guidance.

### 4. STUDY THE BIBLE

- Direct the boys and girls to turn to Genesis 12 in their Bibles. Explain that you will ask questions and tell them where to find the answers in their Bibles. Then fill in the correct answers on their "Fill in the Blank Story."
- Point out the sign "God's Instructions." Note for kids that Abram, his wife Sarai, and his family lived in Ur when God first spoke to him. Ask kids to tell from verse 1 what God told Abram to do. Emphasize the word *go*. Ask where Abram was told to go. Point out that God did not tell Abram exactly where to go, but just to go. Continue with the questions, verses, and comments that follow.
- Look in verses 2-3 to find what God promised to do for Abram. Although God had not told him exactly where to go, Abram obeyed. According to verse 5, who and what did Abram take with him?
- According to verse 7, what did God give to Abram? God promised to give Abram two things: land and children.
- Look in verse 7 to find what Abram did next.
- Direct the kids to turn their chairs so they face the sign "An Agreement." Guide them to locate Genesis 15 in their Bibles. Explain that several years have passed since Abram first received God's promise. Continue with questions, verses, and comments.

- Find God's promise in verse 1. Now, find Abram's question in verse 2. The thing Abram most wanted was children, and God had promised them, but they were not yet born. God re-stated His promise to Abram. He told Abram to count the stars because his descendants would be as numerous as those stars. Look in verse 6 for Abram's response.
- According to Genesis 15:9, what did God tell Abram to gather? God instructed Abram to arrange the animals, split down the middle and opposite each other. That night, a smoking fire pot and a flaming torch appeared! They passed between the divided animals. In verse 18, God promised again to give Abram land.
- Direct kids to face the sign "Three Visitors." Guide kids to locate Genesis 18. Continue with questions, verses, and comments.
- Explain that God changed Abram's name to Abraham and Sarai's name to Sarah. One day Abraham saw three men coming toward him. He rushed out to greet them and invited them to wait while he prepared food. Although Abraham didn't yet realize it, two of the men were actually angels and the third was God! Abraham served food to the visitors under the tree. Find in Genesis 18:9 the question one of them asked Abraham and in verse 10 the promise God made. Sarah was listening in the tent. When she heard the promise that she would have a son, what did she do (v. 12)? Why?
- What did Sarah do when God mentioned that she laughed? (v.15) Read God's response at the end of verse 15. Guide kids to Genesis 21. Ask what happened in verse 3, how old Abraham was according to verse 5, and what Sarah named the child from verse 6.
- Hold up the yarn length again. Remark that God calls us to come to Him. (*Move your finger from one end of the yarn to a spot to designate salvation.*) Then comment that God also tells us, as He did Abraham, that we are to go. (*Move your finger from the middle spot out toward the other end of the yarn.*) Emphasize that we come to God and then we go to tell others.
- Explain that during a lifetime quest, a person moves from who he is at that point to who God wants him to be.
- Remark that Abraham and Sarah may have thought giving them a child was too hard for God since they were both so old. Ask kids what they think might be too hard for God to do. Then read aloud Genesis 18:14. Note that God Himself asked Abraham if anything was too hard for God because He knew the answer was no!

### 5. FOCUS ON THE MEMORY PASSAGE

- Lead the group to read Matthew 7:7 from the poster or to repeat it from memory.
- Reveal Matthew 7:8 and lead kids to read that verse aloud. Ask what kids notice is similar to verse 7. Recall together the letters ASK in helping them to remember the order of the actions in the verse. Call attention to the fact that the actions are repeated in the second verse and are also paired with words meaning the opposites. Some kids may find it helpful to mention the first action as they hold out one hand and then say the opposite word as they hold out the other hand. (asks-->receives)
- Read the two verses together three or four times. Cover the posters. Ask kids to repeat the verses from memory. Emphasize that asking, seeking, and knocking are actions for a lifetime quest with God.

### 6. PRAY

- Tell the kids that right after the three visitors met with Abraham, God explained that the city of Sodom was about to be destroyed. Abraham begged and pleaded with God to spare the people of Sodom who were righteous. God listened to Abraham's prayer and promised to spare the city if as many as 10 righteous people could be found.
- Mention that believers today can pray for others. Suggest the group choose three different groups of people for which they can pray. Explain that the groups might be those who are sick, people of a specific country, or any other kinds of group kids choose. List each of the three choices on a separate, large sheet of paper.
- Point to one of the groups and ask what kids might pray for that group. Suggest kids ask God to move on behalf of the chosen group and to ask Him for specific acts toward the group. Note kids' suggestions on the paper. Continue with the other two groups.
- Form three groups of kids. Give each group a page with the prayer suggestions. Explain that kids in each group will pray for one to two minutes for the group on their sheet. Tell kids that they can then pass the papers to their left and spend time in prayer for the people in the next group. Direct them to pass the papers one more time and pray for the last group.
- Let the kids pray, changing papers every couple of minutes. Add an Amen at the end.

# ENGAGE

- Transition kids into small groups, dividing them into an older group and a younger group. Or, if you have a large group of either older or younger kids, form groups of about 5 or 6 kids. Distribute the Activity Books and pencils.
- Complete pages 14 and 15 together with your group, being sensitive to questions and levels of understanding.
- Complete "Dig Deeper" in this week's Activity Book together.

**ENGAGE ACTIVITY 1: CREATE "GCTGTM" SHELF MINDERS**

**YOU WILL NEED:**

- ☐ "Text Message Abbreviations" (Item 10)
- ☐ Three-by-one-inch paper strips
- ☐ Pens or thin markers
- ☐ Toothpicks
- ☐ Chenille craft stems (3 per student)
- ☐ Glue (or tape)

**TO DO:**

- ☐ Make an example of a Shelf Minder for kids to follow.

- Remind kids that growing closer to God is the adventurous quest of a lifetime. Recall together actions kids can take all through their lives to increase their closeness to God. (Bible reading, praying, obeying God, learning from adults)
- Explain that people sometimes need reminders to keep up their quest. Suggest the kids create text message abbreviations to help them recall what they want to incorporate into their quests. We are going to call these Shelf Minders "reminders you keep on a shelf" to help you grow closer to God.
- Point out that text messages are always brief and use lots of abbreviations, for example LOL for laugh out loud. Show the "Text Message Abbreviations" one at a time and let kids guess what they might mean. Suggest kids think of some text abbreviations of their own.
- Distribute paper strips, toothpicks, pens, and tape or glue. Direct kids to fold the strips in half lengthwise and to write on one side the GCTGTM (Growing Closer to God Text Message) they created. Guide kids to place one end of the toothpick between the folds of the strip and to either glue or tape it in place.

- Give each kid three chenille stems. Demonstrate twisting two stems together to form the head, body, and legs of a human figure. Kids can fold the third chenille stem in half and wrap it around the neck to form arms. Fold in a small section at the end of the arms to make hands. Kids can then bend the figure into a sitting position and fold up the ends of the legs to form feet. Instruct the kids to tape or glue the toothpick signs onto the shelf minder's hands.
- Point out that kids can set the reminders on a shelf, a computer monitor, near a telephone, or any other place they might need a reminder to grow closer to God.

## ENGAGE ACTIVITY 2: PLAY "DRESS THE HIKER" GAME

### YOU WILL NEED:

- ☐ "Dress the Hiker Questions" (Item 11)
- ☐ "Dress the Hiker Chart" (Item 12)
- ☐ "Dress the Hiker Items" (Item 13)
- ☐ Gift bag
- ☐ Two chairs
- ☐ Three half-sheets of construction paper
- ☐ Tape
- ☐ Markers

### TEACHING TIP

If you teach a small group of students, gather the items as suggested but direct the group to work together to completely dress the hiker.

- Call for a volunteer to tell what a quest is. (A search in order to find or get something) Mention that the quest to grow closer to God involves following God's plan.
- Invite the kids to play a game to help them remember important issues about their quests. Show the items you gathered. Ask what these items are most often used for. (Hiking) Place two empty chairs in front of the group and explain that the chairs represent hikers who need to be outfitted. Explain that the group will form two teams and alternate answering questions. When a team answers correctly, one player will choose a colored square from the bag and follow directions on the "Dress a Hiker Chart" as to how many items he may choose from those you gathered. The player will dress his team's chair by taping the items to the chair and play moves to the other team. If a team

cannot correctly answer, play moves to the other team. The first team to have its hiker geared up, wearing at least six items, is the winner.

- Play the game again if time allows. Remind the kids that believers' quests to grow closer to God involve following God's plan and that Abraham's life showed that he spent his life following God's plan for him. Urge the girls and boys to take the challenge of growing closer to God and to remember His promise to help them if they ask.

# EXAMINE

**YOU WILL NEED:**

- ☐ "Dress the Hiker Questions" (Item 11)
- ☐ "Matthew 7:7 Poster" (Item 7)
- ☐ "Matthew 7:8 Poster" (Item 8)
- ☐ Number cube
- ☐ One or two inflated balloons (Having a spare is good!)

- Place the "Dress the Hiker Questions" in three rows of five cards each. Form two teams. One player rolls the number cube to determine how many cards to count. The kid begins counting at the top left corner and counts across the row. The player turns over the card of the number he rolled and reads the question. If his team answers correctly, it keeps the card. If the team does not answer correctly, the card is turned back over. A player from the other team tosses the number cube and begins counting from the card that was turned over. Keep playing until all cards have been answered correctly.
- Remind the group that Abram spent his entire life following God's plan and grew closer to God. Point out believers today can follow Abram's example.
- Pray, asking God to help each kid know how God has led him to the place he is in life and how he can continue to grow closer to God.
- Lead the group to read the memory passage together from the display. Let volunteers repeat the first two verses by memory.
- Kids stand in a circle and tap a balloon around the circle as they repeat the words of Matthew 7:7-8 in order. Continue until the last child is picked up.
- Remind kids to complete this week's daily queries.

## TRUSTING & DEPENDING ON GOD

*Purpose: Through this study kids can...*

**DISCOVER**
how Jesus helped the disciples when they were afraid.

**UNDERSTAND**
that depending on God to overcome fear and other obstacles can bring them closer to God.

**REALIZE**
that God knows what is best even in difficult times.

*Key verse:*
"Who among you, if his son asks him for bread, will give him a stone?"
Matthew 7:9

# EMBARK

**TEACHING TIP**
If you teach a small group of kids, limit the playing space to about 10 square feet (or other small space). Describe only 1 child at a time to freeze in place.

**FREEZE IF I DESCRIBE YOU**

- Welcome kids as they arrive.
- Direct the kids to spread out around the room. Define a boundary for the game that will keep the kids fairly close together.
- Explain that you will call out a description, and kids that you describe must immediately freeze in place while the other kids run around the area avoiding kids frozen in place. If a runner touches a frozen child, he must freeze as well. When you call a different description, all kids are unfrozen unless the new description is also about them.
- Use descriptions such as: kids with brown eyes, kids wearing red, kids in fourth (or other) grade, kids with shoelaces, kids with no buttons on their clothes, kids in church, kids with a missing tooth, kids older than their siblings, and kids with (or without) braces. Change the descriptions often as kids play.
- Point out to the kids that frozen players became obstacles to running kids. Mention that an obstacle is anything that gets in the way of reaching a goal. Explain that people face obstacles all their lives. Those obstacles can keep us from growing closer to God, or we can learn to trust Him to help them overcome the obstacles.
- Explain that the obstacles in the game were just for fun, but some real-life obstacles are important to face.

# EXPLORE

**YOU WILL NEED:**

- ☐ "Bible-Study Assignment Cards" (Item 15)
- ☐ "Learning to Trust Bible Verses" (Item 17)
- ☐ "Learning to Trust Cards" (Item 18)
- ☐ "Matthew 7:9 Poster" (Item 16)

**TEACHING TIP**

Before the lesson, insert the assignment cards in the Bibles at the correct reference. During the STUDY THE BIBLE time, kids can locate the chapter and verse number of their assigned verse.

### 1. INTRODUCE THE QUEST

- Remark to the kids that learning to trust God and to rely on Him happens all along a life-time quest. Explain that this story shows us how even those closest to Jesus struggled to trust Him at times.
- Recall with the kids the five questions they discovered that can help people on their quest of growing closer to God. (Where are you? Who told you that? What are you seeking? Why are you afraid? How much more…?) Encourage kids to listen as you tell the story and discover which of the five questions is part of the story.

### 2. TELL THE BIBLE STORY

***JESUS CALMS THE STORM***
***MATTHEW 8:23-27; MARK 4:37-41 AND LUKE 8:22-25***

*Jesus spent all day teaching crowds of people near the Sea of Galilee. That evening, Jesus wanted to cross over to the other side of the sea. He said, "Let's cross over to the other side of the lake."*

*So Jesus and His disciples left the crowds. They got into a boat and began sailing. Some of the people from the crowds followed in their own boats. While Jesus and His disciples traveled, Jesus fell asleep on a cushion at the back of the boat.*

*All of a sudden, a storm came. The wind was strong, and the waves crashed into the boat. Water was coming into the boat, and the disciples were afraid! Many of the disciples were fishermen. They had survived storms on the sea before, but this storm was different. It was so strong. If the water kept coming in the boat, the boat would sink. Surely they would all drown!*

*The disciples looked to Jesus for help, but Jesus was still fast asleep at the back of the boat. He didn't seem to even notice the storm. Did Jesus care that they were about to sink into the sea?*

*The disciples woke up Jesus. "Lord, save us!" they said. "We are going to die!"*

*Jesus opened His eyes and saw that His friends were afraid. He got up and spoke to the wind. Then Jesus said to the sea, "Silence! Be still!"*

*At the sound of Jesus' voice, the wind stopped blowing and the waves stopped crashing. Everything was calm. The disciples were safe.*

*Jesus looked at His disciples and asked, "Why are you afraid? Do you still have no faith?" Did the disciples not trust Jesus to take care of them?*

*The disciples were amazed. "Who is this man?" they asked each other. "Even the wind and the waves obey Him!"*

## 3. MAKE THE CHRIST CONNECTION

➤ Encourage kids to tell which of the five questions Jesus asks the disciples in the story. Ask, "Why was Jesus not afraid of the storm?" Be sure they understand that Jesus has all power over everything. Note for kids that Jesus not only can control nature, but He also has power over any other obstacle people face, such as fearing the death of family members, feeling rejected by other people, and being angry at circumstances.

## 4. STUDY THE BIBLE

➤ Point out that even Jesus' disciples faced difficult obstacles.

➤ Form teams and give each team a Bible with an assignment card inside. Let the teams locate their verses and determine answers to their questions. Call on the teams to share their findings.

➤ Continue with these questions and comments:

- Ask, "What do you think of when you think about storms?"
- Emphasize the danger the disciples were in. Mention that many of the disciples were experienced sailors who made their living fishing. Note that the storm was so fierce that even they feared the boat would sink.
- Ask, "What is Jesus doing during the storm?" Direct the kids to Luke 8:24. Ask, "How do we know the disciples are afraid?"
- Read Mark 4:39 aloud to the kids. Ask, "What is told in this verse that is not told in Luke 8:24?" Note that as soon as Jesus speaks to the storm, all is calm.
- You might expect the disciples to be all smiles by now. However, what do Luke 8:25 and Mark 4:41 say? Why are the men still fearful?
- Jesus asks the men a question. Read Mark 4:40 to find what it is.
- Recall with the kids the five questions they discovered that can help people on their quest of growing closer to God. (Where are you? Who told you that? What are you seeking? Why are you afraid? How much more…?)
- Remind the kids that one of the questions was about what people are afraid of. Point out that Jesus asked the disciples that question when they feared the storm. Note that the disciples did not yet understand and trust that Jesus was in control of everything.

### 5. FOCUS ON THE MEMORY VERSE

- Ask what things kids like them might fear. List their answers on a large sheet of paper. If kids need help getting started, ask what the disciples feared in today's Bible story and ask whether people today have the same fear.
- Explain that God does not always remove whatever we fear, but He does promise to be with us as we face what we fear. He wants people to trust Him with their fears, to remember His presence, and trust Him every step of the way.
- Direct kids to read the "Mathew 7:9 Poster" together. Ask a child to explain the meaning of the verse to the group. Explain to kids that the question in the verse is supposed to sound unbelievable, just as it is unbelievable that God would not give a good thing when His people ask for something.
- Remind kids that just like a father loves to give good gifts to his children, God, our heavenly Father, wants to give good gifts to us, His children. We can always trust God to know what is best for us, even in difficult times.

**6. PRAY**

- Distribute the "Learning to Trust Bible Verses." Kids may work in pairs to locate their assigned Bible verses. When students have found the verses, ask them to read silently to find out how they can learn to trust God.
- Call on one kid to select a "Learning to Trust Card." Read the card aloud and ask kids to decide who has the Bible verse that relates to the statement on the card. Continue until each Bible verse has been matched to a statement.
- Point out that each verse can help people know how to trust or depend on God.
- Spread the "Learning to Trust Cards" before the group. Ask, "What might be the hardest action to take when learning to trust God?"
- After several responses, mention that God knows which of these are hardest, which are easiest, and which each person needs most. Suggest each kid silently choose one of the ways to trust God and to cross her ankles when a choice has been made.
- Urge the kids to silently ask God to help them learn to trust Him more through the way they chose.
- Sit quietly as kids pray silently their prayers. After a few moments, add a quiet *Amen*.

# ENGAGE

**YOU WILL NEED:**
- ☐ Activity Books
- ☐ Pencils

- Transition kids into small groups (an older and younger group). Distribute Activity Books and pencils. Guide kids to complete activities on pages 20 and 21.
- Review the "Dig Deeper" activity and discuss what kids have learned about growing closer to God.

## ENGAGE ACTIVITY 1: MAKE "TRUTH SPINNERS"

**YOU WILL NEED:**

- ☐ Large marbles (one per kid)
- ☐ Used CDs (one per kid)
- ☐ "CD Templates" (Item 19)
- ☐ Plain paper
- ☐ Permanent markers and pencils
- ☐ Scissors
- ☐ Tape

**TEACHING TIP**

If you are pressed for time, let the kids draw directly on the shiny sides of the CDs rather than making and decorating the paper circles.

- ➤ Suggest the kids make fun spinners to help them recall actions they want to do in order to move forward on their quest of closeness to God.
- ➤ Distribute "CD Template" to each child. Guide the kids to cut out the circles. Cut out the small circle in the middle of the CD. Instruct kids to print on the circles three things they can do to increase their dependence on God. Let kids add various decorations. Attach circles to the CDs with tape loops.
- ➤ Demonstrate using the spinners by placing a CD on top of a marble and then twirling the top of the marble showing through the hole in the CD. Spinning the marbles on a smooth surface such as a table or tile floor will increase the amount of time the CDs will spin. Let kids time their spinners or compete with each other to find out which one will spin longest.
- ➤ Instruct kids to hold their CDs still. Comment that kids can use their spinners for fun, but that the spinners can also remind them that they are on the adventure of a lifetime — closeness to God!
- ➤ Sometimes people wonder why God does not stop all problems or obstacles in the world? One reason might be so people can learn to trust God though the problem or obstacle. God has other important lessons for us to learn. Others need to see how believers trust Jesus during problem times. But know this: God sees every obstacle in your life and promises to be with you through all difficult times you face. You can trust what He says.
- ➤ Read aloud to the group Joshua 1:9b. Point out that God provides other people to help during times of difficulty — parents, teachers, pastors, and others.

## ENGAGE ACTIVITY 2: DRAW IN THE DARK

**YOU WILL NEED:**
- ☐ A large sheet of paper for each group of three kids
- ☐ Markers or pens
- ☐ Tape
- ☐ A blindfold for each group

**TO DO:**
- ☐ Tape each sheet of paper to the wall, spread out around the room. Place one or two markers and a blindfold near each paper.

**TEACHING TIP**

Need more blindfolds? Use sleep masks, scarves, or men's ties.

➤ Form groups of three. Assign each group to sit beside a different paper on the wall. Ask one person in each group to draw lines dividing the paper into three equal spaces. Quietly whisper to those kids, telling them to draw a simple picture of a lake in one blank section on their paper. Urge kids not to tell their groups what they are drawing.

➤ Explain to the whole group that their team members will draw a picture, and their team must figure out what they have drawn. Comment that the drawers will have 30 seconds to draw their pictures, but they will be drawing in the dark.

➤ Assist kids who are drawing to put on blindfolds. Help the drawing child place the marker inside one of the sections on the paper. Instruct the rest of the kids to sit with their backs to the person drawing. Time 30 seconds as the kid draws. At the end of time, the kids who will be guessing turn to face the picture. Allow 30 seconds for kids to guess what the drawing represents. Tell the correct answer if needed. Repeat the process letting other kids in the group draw. For these next rounds, use the words boat and then storm.

➤ After each child has a turn to draw, ask the group what the words have in common. (*All came from the today's Bible story.*)

➤ Encourage the group to name facts from the story of Jesus calming the storm. Each time someone names a different fact, make a tally mark on a sheet of paper. If kids need help, let them locate the story in their Bibles in Mark 4:37-41 and Luke 8:22-25. Recall together the obstacle the disciples faced during the storm. (*Fear*) Ask why they did not need to be afraid. (*Jesus is in control.*)

➤ Say: "Fear is not the only obstacle people might face in their quest for closeness to God." Kids may form new groups and make new drawings representing things that are obstacles to people moving closer to God. Use these drawing assignments and talk about why they can be obstacles: fear, anger.

# EXAMINE

**YOU WILL NEED:**

- ☐ "Climb the Mountain" (Item 20)
- ☐ Paper plates
- ☐ A marker
- ☐ Tape

**TO DO:**

- ☐ Tape the "Climb the Mountain" game sheets to a wall, forming a zig-zag trail from the floor as high as the tallest kids in the group can reach.
- ☐ Print Matthew 7:9 on two sets of paper plates, three or four words per plate. Tape one set of plates to the walls in mixed up order and as far from each other as possible in your setting.

**TEACHING TIP**

To help younger readers identify the words on the plates, print each set of words in different colors or on different colored plates.

- ➤ Explain that kids will work together to overcome obstacles on their quest to reach the top of the mountain. Place the mountain climber on the first space. Invite a kid to choose a number card and advance the climber that number of spaces on the path. After the kid returns the number to the bag, he answers the question printed in the space or does what is printed. Play moves to the next kid in the group. Continue in the same manner until the mountain climber reaches the top of the mountain.
- ➤ If time allows, play the game again. Turn the papers to face the wall. Explain that this time kids must tell a fact from the Bible story, tell an obstacle that might keep someone from growing closer to God, or tell a way to learn to trust God. Place the mountain climber on the lowest paper. Call on a player to tell his answer and move the mountain climber up one space. The next player must give a different answer in order to advance the mountain climber. Continue taking turns until the mountain climber is at the top of the mountain.
- ➤ Form a circle. Remind the boys and girls that prayer is an important action in the quest for closeness to God.

- Call for prayer requests that the kids want the group to pray about. Ask for volunteers to pray aloud for each request. If no child responds, pray for the request yourself.
- End the prayer by asking God to help each kid in the group to learn how to trust God more.
- Assign one child to be the caller. Give this child a set of paper plates (Make sure this child is a strong reader) Other kids line up one behind the other. The caller reads the first three words from Matthew 7:9 and holds up the corresponding plate. The first player runs to touch the plate with those words and runs back to the group. The caller reads the first six (or seven) words of the verse and holds up the two corresponding plates. The second player runs to touch the first plate and then to touch the second one. The caller reads the words for the first three plates and holds them up. The next child in line runs to the three plates in order. Play continues in the same manner until the verse is complete and/or each kid has had a turn to run.
- Continue the game by choosing another caller. Explain that you will time the group and will announce how long it takes for the group to finish running the verse. Play the same way as before. Encourage the kids to finish faster each time.
- For the next round of the game, instruct kids to run the entire verse without hearing it read first. Time how long it takes the group to finish. Try to get faster each time.
- For more of a challenge, kids can change the order of the plates between rounds. Or, add plates with the words of Matthew 7:7-8 to the walls and let kids run all three verses.
- Play until the last child is picked up.

# The Quest & Difficult Times

## CLINGING CLOSE TO GOD

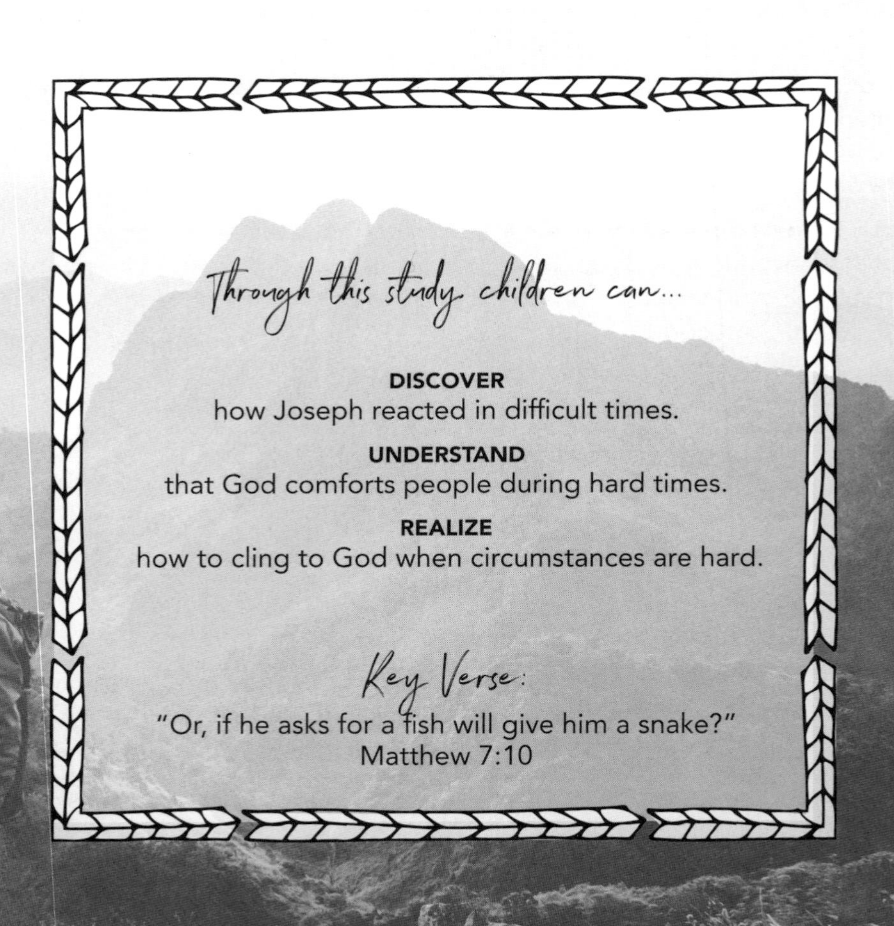

*Through this study, children can...*

**DISCOVER**
how Joseph reacted in difficult times.

**UNDERSTAND**
that God comforts people during hard times.

**REALIZE**
how to cling to God when circumstances are hard.

*Key Verse:*
"Or, if he asks for a fish will give him a snake?"
Matthew 7:10

# EMBARK

**YOU WILL NEED:**

- [ ] Masking tape

**TO DO:**

- [ ] Make a long tape line on the floor. The line should be long enough for kids to stand one behind the other on it.

**WHAT I LIKE BEST**

- Greet kids as they arrive. Invite the kids to stand straddling the tape line, one behind the other.
- Explain that you will name a choice kids might make and tell what kids should do to indicate which choice they would make. Tell kids to take one step to the left if they like birthdays best or to take one step to the right if they like Christmas best. After kids respond, ask kids to tell why they chose the one they did. Continue with these other choices and directing kids how to respond:
- Take three baby steps to the right if you like vacations best or three baby steps to the left if you like sleepovers best.
- Take a giant step left if you like playing in water best or a giant step right if you like playing in sand best.
- Take one jump to the left if you like riding bikes best or one jump to the right if you like roller-blading best.
- Turn to the right if you like watching movies best or turn to the left if you like playing outside best.
- Leap to the right if you like winning games best or leap to the left if you like winning races best.
- Take two regular steps left if you like staying up late best or two regular steps right if you like getting up early best.
- Explain that these choices were fun things to do. Ask how they feel when things happen that are not fun and cannot be changed. Say that the Bible tells about people who experienced difficult times and how they dealt with those times.
- Open your Bible and read John 16:33. Jesus said everyone would have trouble during their lives, but that Jesus promised to be with His followers and to give them peace as they go through trouble.

# EXPLORE

**YOU WILL NEED:**

- ☐ "Difficult Situations" (Item 21)
- ☐ Plain paper
- ☐ Marker
- ☐ "Matthew 7:7 Poster" (Item 7)
- ☐ "Matthew 7:8 Poster" (Item 8)
- ☐ "Matthew 7:9 Poster" (Item 16)
- ☐ "Matthew 7:10 Poster" (Item 22)

**TO DO:**

- ☐ Display the first three verses of the Memory Passage near the front of the group.

### 1. INTRODUCE THE QUEST

➤ Explain that in today's lesson we will understand that God comforts people during hard times. Mention that people today also experience difficult times or events that are hard to deal with. Suggest the group listen to these short stories and decide what hard or difficult situation the person in the story must put up with. Read the stories aloud. Between the readings, ask kids what the difficulty is. Print kids' responses on the paper.

➤ Be sensitive to kids' responses to these situations. Some kids may have experienced some of them and be reminded of their fears, insecurities, and pain. Others may become overly concerned that some situations might happen to them in the future. Omit any stories you feel might cause more harm than good for the group to hear and discuss.

### 2. TELL THE BIBLE STORY

➤ Explain that in today's Bible story we will discover how Joseph reacted in difficult times. This quest spans several chapters of Genesis as it tells the story of Joseph's life. Note for kids that parts of the story are about good things that happened to Joseph and parts are about bad things that happened.

➤ Suggest the kids sit with both feet flat on the floor when they hear good things happening, cross their feet like an X when they hear bad things, and cross one knee over the other with things are neither good nor bad. Tell the following story in your own words with your Bible open to Genesis 37.

**JOSEPH'S LIFE**
**PASSAGES SELECTED IN GENESIS 37–50**

2. *Joseph was born to Jacob and Rachael and had 11 brothers. When Joseph was 17 years old, his job was to help his brothers care for the sheep.* (cross one knee over the other)

*Jacob loved Joseph more than his other children. He gave Joseph a beautiful robe of many colors.* (sit with both feet flat on the floor) *The brothers were jealous. Joseph told his family about dreams he had where he was a ruler over them. That just made them more jealous.* good

*One day, the brothers saw Joseph coming and decided to kill him.* (cross feet like an X) *They threw him in a pit and considered what to do. Finally, they sold Joseph as a slave to a group on its way to Egypt. The brothers rubbed goat blood on Joseph's coat and used it to convince their father that Joseph was dead.* bad

*When Joseph got to Egypt, he was sold as a slave to Potiphar, the captain of the guard. God was with Joseph and made everything he did successful.* (sit with both feet flat on the floor) *Soon Joseph was in charge of everything Potiphar owned. However, Potiphar's wife told him a terrible lie about Joseph. Potiphar was so angry, he had Joseph thrown in jail.* (cross feet like an X) good bad

*God was with Joseph in the jail. He caused the jailer to like Joseph. Soon Joseph was in charge of all the prisoners in the jail.* (sit with both feet flat on the floor) *One day two men in the jail had dreams that Joseph explained for them.* (cross one knee over the other) *Later one of the men remembered that Joseph could tell about dreams. He told Pharaoh about Joseph and Joseph was called to Pharaoh's court.* good

*With God's help, Joseph successfully told Pharaoh about his dream and the coming famine.* (sit with both feet flat on the floor) *Pharaoh put Joseph in charge of everything in Egypt so that his country could survive the famine that was to come. Pharaoh made Joseph second in command over all of Egypt. He gave Joseph a ring, a robe, and a gold chain—symbols of the power that he was handing over to Joseph.* good good

*The famine spread all the way back to Joseph's home in Canaan. His father Jacob sent ten of the brothers to Egypt to get food.* (cross one knee over the other) *They had no idea they would be asking Joseph for what they needed! Joseph*

*recognized his brothers, but they didn't recognize him. Joseph tested them and found they had become trustworthy men. When he told them who he was, he invited them to bring the whole family to live in Egypt where he could be sure they had food.* (sit with both feet flat on the floor)

*The whole family moved to Egypt. Jacob and Joseph were so glad to see each other again and rejoiced that God provided for them. After many years, Jacob died. Joseph's brothers worried that Joseph would harm them in revenge for what they had done to him.* (cross feet like an X) *Instead, Joseph said, "Don't be afraid. You planned evil for me, but God planned it for good. See the survival of so many people! Don't be afraid. I will take care of you."* (sit with both feet flat on the floor)

### 3. MAKE THE CHRIST CONNECTION

➤ Invite the kids to tell some of the good things that happened during the story. Then ask what some of the bad things were. Ask which of those bad things Joseph could have kept from happening. (*None*)

➤ Remind kids that God wants us to realize how to cling to him when circumstances are hard. Encourage kids to remember from meeting one that one reason there are hard things in our lives is because of the broken world we live in because of sin. Point out that Jesus promised to make all things right in the end, to be with His people, and to give peace.

### 4. STUDY THE BIBLE

➤ Assure kids that God can comfort people during any hard times they face. Direct half of the kids locate and read Joshua 1:9 while the other half locates and reads John 14:27. Help kids understand that one way God helps during difficult times is by being with the person and by giving His peace—a kind of peace no one else can give. Remark that God sometimes comforts people by sending other people to help them out of the situation or to go through the situation with them. Point out that sometimes God provides help through trusted adults who can protect kids from harmful situations. Note for kids that these are just some of the ways God might comfort people through hard times. Emphasize that God promises His presence no matter where He leads His people.

➤ Explain that one title God is sometimes given is that of Judge. Read aloud to the kids the question written in Genesis 18:25. Encourage the kids to find Revelation 21:4-7 in their Bibles to find what God, the Judge, promises will happen.

## 5. FOCUS ON THE MEMORY PASSAGE

- Refer to the Matthew 7:7 Poster and ask what memory tip helps them recall this verse. (ASK: Ask, Seek, Knock.) Read the verse together one time. Repeat it by memory together one time. Recall for kids that doing what Jesus' describes in this memory passage is one way to grow closer to God.
- Refer to the Matthew 7:8 Poster and inquire how ASK can help recall this verse. (*Opposites: ask/receive; seek/find; knock/opened.*) Lead the group to read the verse together one time, repeat it by memory one time, and then to repeat both verses by memory one time.
- Call attention to the Matthew 7:9 Poster. Remind kids that the question in the verse is supposed to sound unbelievable, just as it is unbelievable that God would not give a good thing when His people ask for something. Read the verse together one time. Repeat it by memory. Repeat all three verses together by memory.
- Display the Matthew 7:10 Poster. Emphasize that this question is much like the question in verse 9. It is another example of being unbelievable that a parent would give a snake instead of a fish, and that it is just as unbelievable that God would do such a thing. Practice the verse a few times before leading the group to repeat the entire passage by memory.

## 6. PRAY

- Remind kids that prayer is an important way to grow closer to God, especially when going through difficult times. Emphasize that God always hears prayers even though He may answer them in different ways than people think He will.
- Allow kids to share any prayer concerns they have. Encourage kids to pray about any hard times they may be experiencing themselves and to remember that God hears those prayers and will answer them.
- Invite kids to close their eyes to help them concentrate and to keep their hands to themselves. Explain that when we pray, we always want to keep the attention on Jesus and not on ourselves. Explain that you will mention something kids can pray about and then wait as kids pray silently to God.
- Use prayer suggestions such as these: Thank God for something good in your life. (*Pause a few seconds as kids pray.*) If you need to tell God you are sorry about anything, do that. If not, ask Him to help you keep obeying Him. (*Pause.*) Praise God for being more powerful than anyone or anything else. (*Pause.*) Ask God to help anyone you know who needs His help. (*Pause.*) Ask God for any help you need. (*Pause.*) Amen.

# ENGAGE

- Transition kids into small groups, dividing them into an older group and younger group. Distribute Activity Books and pencils. Guide kids to complete pages 26 and 27 in their Activity Books.
- Review what kids have learned today. Take this opportunity to explain Bible truths and to go deeper into the Bible study.

## ENGAGE ACTIVITY 1: MAKE "MY QUEST PAPER GLIDERS"

**YOU WILL NEED:**

- ☐ Plastic drinking straws
- ☐ Paper clips
- ☐ 1-by-9-inch paper strips
- ☐ 1-by-6-inch paper strips
- ☐ Pens or thin markers
- ☐ Scissors

- Remind kids that the lifetime quest of growing closer to God will involve clinging to Him during hard times as well as good times.
- Encourage kids to name ways they can grow closer to God during difficult situations. If needed, refer to what kids learned during Group Time or as they worked their Activity Book pages.
- Suggest the group make paper gliders with reminders of the actions they just named. Lead the kids to follow these instructions:
- On one large paper strip, print at least two ways to grow closer to God even when times are hard. (For example, "Remembering God is with me.")
- On one shorter strip, print My Quest: Growing Closer to God.
- Slide one paper clip into an end of a straw with the narrower part of the clip on the inside and the wider part on the outside of the straw. Add another paper clip to the other end of the straw.
- Connect the two ends of the large paper strip together to form a circle and slide it into one of the paper clips. Do the same thing with the other strip.
- Be sure that the paper circles line up one behind the other.
- Before kids fly their gliders, ask them to tell the group the ways they printed on their gliders. After everyone has shared, let kids line up shoulder to shoulder and launch their gliders. Explain that a good way to

launch is to hold the straw in the middle with the smaller circler in the front and to gently push it forward rather than throwing it.

- Help kids make adjustments as needed by making larger or smaller circles with the paper strips. Before launching the gliders the next time, encourage the kids to say one or more verses of the memory passage for this study.
- Allow kids to toss their gliders several times. Call the group back together. Remark that the gliders are fun to fly but are also to remind the kids that they can cling to God no matter what is happening in their lives.

## ENGAGE ACTIVITY 2: CREATE "JOSEPH'S JOURNAL ENTRIES"

**YOU WILL NEED:**

- ☐ Paper (lined is best but any will work)
- ☐ Pens or pencils

- Ask the kids why people keep journals. One reason may be to express personal feelings that they want to keep private. Note that journals are also kept to remind people of events that happened. Point out that journals are written in first person and tell about events and feelings.
- Suggest the kids create a journal about Joseph and the things, both good and bad that happened to him. Distribute paper and pens or pencils.
- Talk together about what events happened to Joseph as a young person. These could include his father giving him a robe, tattling on his brothers, telling his dreams to his family, being tossed into a pit, and sold to a group headed to Egypt. Kids may choose to each create a journal entry for a different event or to all write about the same event and see how different they turn out. Younger kids can also draw a picture of the different events.
- Allow a few minutes for kids to work. Let them share their entries. Ask what Joseph could have done to help him cling to God even when things were hard.
- Continue with another section or two of Joseph's life, such as being in jail because someone lied about him, being put in charge of the food for the whole country of Egypt, finding out his brothers were in Egypt, or others you choose. Allow time for kids to make additional journal entries. Let kids write about other events from Joseph's life as time allows.
- Consider together difficult situations kids might have. Invite each student to write a journal entry as though they were experiencing a difficult situation and what they might feel and do. Discuss these entries and encourage kids to add ways the person in the situation could grow closer to God.

# EXAMINE

**YOU WILL NEED:**
- ☐ "Joseph's Life Cards" (Item 23)
- ☐ Plain paper
- ☐ Markers or pens
- ☐ A numbered cube

➤ Gather kids together and call on volunteers to tell good things that happened to Joseph in the Bible story. Then ask them to name things that seemed bad that happened. Emphasize that in each bad thing, God was placing Joseph in the right spot for what would happen next.

➤ Kids will work together to continue reviewing today's Bible story. Explain that one child will pick one of the "Joseph's Life Cards" and then act out one word on the card at a time without speaking. Note for kids that when someone guesses the word, their team gets 100 points. If the player can tell how the verse was important in the Bible story, the team will get 300 more points. Call for a volunteer to be the first one to choose a card and act out the letters of the word on the card like charades. After using all the cards, ask whether any kids want to try forming acting out letters of other words from the Bible story. Let volunteers take turns.

➤ Emphasize to kids that Joseph could have spent his time wondering why God was letting him suffer and sit pouting, but instead chose to obey God and move on in obedience to God. Urge boys and girls to remember that God has promised to make all things right eventually, that He loves them, and that He is always present with them.

➤ Encourage the children to think of any hard/difficult times they are facing or that someone they know is facing. Tell the group that you will time one minute as kids pause and pray for whoever they thought about. Guide them to consider praying that God will give comfort, strength to endure, and remembrance of God's presence. Say a quiet *Amen* at the end of the minute.

- Lead the group to read together the first four verses of the Memory Passage, Matthew 7:7-10. Suggest the kids start with the first word and work together to form the letters of that word. Instruct them to continue on through the four verses as they wait to be picked up.
- Remind kids to complete this week's daily queries in the Younger or Older Kids Activity Book.

# The Quest & Others

## GROWING CLOSER TO GOD THROUGH SERVICE

*Through this study children can...*

**DISCOVER**
that Jesus is faithful to forgive and to redeem.

**UNDERSTAND**
that serving others is living like Jesus.

**REALIZE**
they can decide to follow Jesus throughout their life-long quest.

*Key verse:*

"If you then, who are evil, know how to give good gifts to your children, how much more will your Father in heaven give good things to those who ask Him!"
Matthew 7:11

# EMBARK

**YOU WILL NEED:**

- [ ] Large disposable cups
- [ ] Popped popcorn (or ping pong balls or packing peanuts)
- [ ] Two large bowls or buckets
- [ ] Masking tape

**TO DO:**

- [ ] Make two tape lines as far apart as practical in your space. Consider using a hallway if your meeting area is unusable for the game.

**TEACHING TIP**

If you have a small group, play with one line of kids. Time the group and then encourage them to play again, trying to finish in less time. If you have a large group, form teams of 5 to 6 and place a bowl for each team at the tape line.

**MAY I SERVE YOU?**

➤ Welcome kids as they arrive. Form two teams. Direct each team to line up, one behind the other, with the first player at one tape line. Place a stack of cups and a container of popcorn near the last player on the team. Place a bowl directly across from each team at the other tape line.

➤ Explain to kids that the last player in line will ask the player in front of him, "May I serve you?" That player asks the player in front of him, and so on until the player at the tape line answers, "Yes." Kids pass the answer back down the line. When it reaches the last player, he scoops popcorn into a cup and passes it in front of him. Other players pass it to the first player who places the cup on his head and proceeds to walk quickly to the bowl for his team. He dumps the popcorn into the bowl and runs to the back of his team's line. Now he is the one asking "May I serve you?" Tell kids that when the last player on the team completes his turn, all members of the team sit down. Note for kids that they can keep their hands close to the cups on their heads but may not hold onto them. If the cup falls, the kid picks it up and continues on his way without stopping to put any popcorn back in the cup.

➤ Once all teams are seated, the team with the most in its bowl wins the race.

➤ Emphasize that serving others helps people grow closer to God because they are living in the way Jesus lived.

# EXPLORE

**YOU WILL NEED:**
- ☐ The memory passage posters from previous sessions (Items 7, 8, 16, and 22)
- ☐ Matthew 7:11 Poster" (Item 24)
- ☐ Index cards
- ☐ Pen or marker
- ☐ (Section #2) "Breakfast with Jesus Story Strips" (Item 25)
- ☐ (Section #2) Tape
- ☐ (Section #4) "Serving Others Spinners" (Item 26)
- ☐ (Section #6) "Group Prayer" (Item 27)

**TO DO:**
- ☐ Print each word of Matthew 7:11 on a different index card.
- ☐ Display the posters in the area for group time.
- ☐ (Section #2) Tape each story strip beneath a different chair. (For smaller groups, place more than one beneath each chair.)

**TEACHING TIP**
(Section #2) If you do not use chairs, tape the strips around the room.

### 1. INTRODUCE THE QUEST

➤ Explain that in today's lesson we will discover that serving others is living like Jesus. Mention that today's Bible story takes place after Jesus' death and resurrection. Note for kids that Jesus had in fact already appeared to the disciples several times. (John 21:1) Remark that on this particular day, the disciples had been fishing without catching anything. When they obeyed Jesus and threw their nets out on the other side of the boat, they caught 153 fish! (John 21:11) Explain that when Peter realized Jesus was on the shore, he jumped out of the boat and swam to shore. When all the disciples joined them, they ate a breakfast of fish and bread. (John 21:7-13)

### 2. TELL THE BIBLE STORY

➤ Invite the kids to look for the strips taped beneath their chair seats. Explain that they can help tell today's Bible story as they read the strips aloud in order. Encourage the kids to read loud enough that everyone can clearly hear them.

**BREAKFAST WITH JESUS**
**JOHN 21:15-25**

*Jesus asked Peter, "Do you love Me more than these?"*
*Peter answered, "Yes Lord. You know I love You."*
*"Feed my lambs," Jesus said.*
*Again Jesus asked Peter, "Son of John, do you love Me?"*
*"You know I love You," Peter answered.*
*"Take care of My sheep," Jesus said.*
*"Simon, do you love Me?" Jesus asked.*
*Peter was hurt that Jesus asked him this question a third time. "You know everything, Lord," he said. "You know I love You."*

*"Feed my sheep. When you were young, you took care of yourself. When you are old, you will need help to take care of yourself."*

*Jesus wanted Peter to know how he would glorify God. Then Jesus said, "Follow Me."*

*(Leader continues from here.) When Peter looked around and saw John following them, he asked Jesus, "What about him?"*

*Jesus said, "If I want him to live until I come back, what is that to you. YOU follow Me."*

*Jesus didn't say that John would live that long. He just meant that it was not Peter's business.*

*John wrote that Jesus did so many things that if they were written down, the world could not hold them all!*

## 3. MAKE A CHRIST CONNECTION

- Invite a volunteer to circle the words "how much more" in the displayed memory passage.
- Remind the kids that "how much more" was the last of the five questions they read in the first meeting of this study. Explain that even human fathers will rarely give their children bad things when they ask for good things. Note for kids that Jesus is pointing out that if humans will do that, then our good God would do so much more.
- Emphasize that people can trust that God will give His children more good than they can imagine. They can trust it because Jesus, God's only Son, said it.

## 4. STUDY THE BIBLE

- Ask kids what they think Jesus meant when He told Peter to feed His sheep. Help the girls and boys realize that Jesus wanted Peter to serve others.
- Call for ideas of other words that mean the same or nearly the same as serve. Expect answers such as help, aid, assist, lend a hand, wait on, care for, tend to, and others. Be sure to allow thinking time before adding your own answers.
- Place the two spinners before the group. Allow two different volunteers to spin the spinners. Ask the group to tell how they could serve the person named on one spinner using the item named on the other spinner. Continue with other kids taking turns spinning the spinner.
- Remove the spinner with items shown on it. Allow a kid to spin the other spinner. Ask the group to tell additional ways, besides those named earlier, to serve the person named on the spinner. Continue in this way for three or four spins.
- Emphasize that when people serve others, they are living the way Jesus lived, something very pleasing to God.
- Ask kids why Jesus might have asked Peter three times if he loved Jesus. Remind kids as necessary that Peter had denied Jesus three times the night before his crucifixion. Peter was sorry about what he had done, and he still loved Jesus. And Jesus loved Peter. He loved him enough to forgive him for what he had done. Urge kids to remember that God can and will forgive any sin.

## 5. FOCUS ON THE MEMORY VERSE

- Lead the kids to read the memory passage from the display.
- Instruct boys and girls to stand in a circle. Call for a volunteer to stand in the middle of the circle. Distribute the word cards. Some kids may hold more than one card if you have fewer kids than cards. If you have more kids than cards, some children may share cards.
- At your signal, the person inside the circle begins patting his legs and kids in the circle begin passing the cards to the right. As long as the person in the middle is patting his legs, kids in the circle pass the cards. When the patter in the middle stops, the passing stops.
- Cards must then be read in their correct order. Kids may refer to the Matthew 7:11 Poster as needed.
- After the verse has been repeated several times, remove the poster and play again.

- Lead the kids to read the entire memory passage from the display. Remove the first poster. Encourage boys and girls to repeat the first verse by memory and then read the rest of the passage. Remove the second poster. Kids will repeat by memory the first two verses of the passage and read the rest. Continue, removing one poster each time until kids repeat the entire passage by memory.

**6. PRAY**

- Place the Group Prayer papers on the floor where all kids can see them.
- Point out to kids the order the papers will be read. Ask for volunteers to read the different solo parts. Mention that everyone will read the parts labeled *All*. Explain this group prayer is a real prayer to God and should be read respectfully and sincerely.
- Call on the first volunteer to read the first solo. Continue through the prayer.

# ENGAGE

- Transition kids into small groups, dividing them into an older group and a younger group. Distribute Activity Books and pencils.
- Guide kids to complete pages 38 and 39 in their Activity Books, digging deeper into this week's Bible truths.

### ENGAGE ACTIVITY 1: MAIL A MESSAGE IN A BOTTLE

**YOU WILL NEED:**

- ☐ Clean, dry, empty plastic bottles with lids (Sports drink bottles with wide lids will work well for this activity)
- ☐ Paper
- ☐ Markers or pens
- ☐ Paper clips
- ☐ Ribbon
- ☐ Confetti
- ☐ Adhesive-backed mailing labels

**TO DO:**

- ☐ Remove all labels from the bottles.

**TEACHING TIP**
Additional Items to consider including: chapstick, smarties, dumdums, combs or small hygiene items. Plain paper and packing tape can be substituted for the mailing labels. Confetti can be made from shredded paper or purchased. OPTION: Make several of the bottles and deliver them to a food pantry, family shelter, or soup kitchen to be given away to those who need encouragement. According to the U.S. Post Office, these bottles may be mailed as packages. However, be advised that they may get crushed in the mail. Avoid putting anything inside the bottles that might be a problem if the bottle is crushed.

- Remark that serving others is not only living like Jesus did but is also showing our deep love for Him.
- Ask kids to name people they have seen serving (helping) other people. Expect answers such as friends, first responders, parents, teachers, and others. Ask kids then to name people groups who might need someone to serve or help them. Possibilities are those who are sick, lonely, hurt, hungry, afraid, sad, or unable to complete something without help.
- Mention that encouraging people when they are facing difficult situations is one way to serve or help others. Explain that Bible verse cards, interesting pictures of God's creation, and happy notes can help people in many situations to feel better.
- Suggest the group make special messages to put inside clear bottles and mail to people who are unable to attend church. Mention that senior adults sometimes get to the point they cannot drive to church or they have physical problems that make sitting a long time painful or impossible. Note for kids that sometimes other kids cannot come to church because their parents have other plans or don't want to bring them.
- After kids write their messages, guide them to tightly roll the messages (tight enough to fit inside the mouth of the bottle) and to attach paper clips to each end of the rolls. Direct kids to tie yarn or ribbon tightly around the middle of the message and then remove the paper clips. Kids may slide the messages inside the bottles. Suggest kids add a few sprinkles of confetti and some strips of narrow curling ribbon. Kids might also want to include small shells or other small objects.
- When everything has been placed in the bottle, screw the cap back on it. Secure it with packing tape. Print the name and address of the recipient on a mailing label and attach the label to the bottle. Explain that kids can take the bottles to the post office and mail them just as they are.
- Lead girls and boys to hold their bottles and to pray for the persons that will receive them.

## ENGAGE ACTIVITY 2: BE SERVANTS TO OTHERS

- Ask girls and boys to tell examples of Jesus helping others. Remind them that when they help or serve others, they are living as Jesus did, which pleases Him. Remark that serving others helps a person grow closer to God because they are acting in obedience to Him.
- Lead the group in one of the following acts of service or another one that fits your situation.
- Serve soldiers: Prepare care boxes with hot chocolate packets, letter-writing materials, stamps, puzzle books, lip balm, hand sanitizer, and other comfort items. Be sure to include a card with a hand-written message thanking the soldiers for their service and a Bible verse, such as John 3:16. Wrap the boxes and address them. If you have a local military base, take the boxes there. If not, contact a local military recruiting office for suggestion for the best place to send the boxes.
- Throw a birthday party for someone at a retirement center, nursing home, or a community center. Work together to decorate cookies or a cake. Make birthday cards. Make or gather decorations. Provide balloons. Provide a Bible for kids to write encouraging notes on the fly leaf and present to the honoree. Pray that the person to whom you are throwing the party will know God's love through the love the kids show.
- Make fleece blankets for a retirement center or for a police department to distribute in crisis situations. Kids can work in pairs or groups of four to make these simple blankets. Starting with a 4-by-5-foot length of fleece, let kids cut slits around all four sides (about inch wide and four inches long). After cutting, tie each pair of fringe strips in a square knot. Go all the way around the blanket tying the strips. (If you have an odd number of strips, just cut one in half and tie both halves together.) Kids can add cards with Bible verses or personal prayers for the recipient. Fold the blankets. Pin on the cards. Let kids help deliver the blankets if possible.
- Help public servants cool off. Kids can print messages on adhesive-backed labels and apply them to new, unopened water bottles. Take kids to a fire station, police station, or post office to deliver them.
- Be sure an adult accompanies any child serving others. Lead kids in praying for the people whom they help.
- Finally, encourage kids to watch at home, school, and in their community they go to notice people who need their help. Note for kids that when they help, they are living as Jesus did.

# EXAMINE

**YOU WILL NEED:**
- ☐ "Meeting 5 Review Questions" for this meeting (Item 28)
- ☐ Sandwich-sized zip-top bags
- ☐ Hand sanitizer
- ☐ Scoops (about 1/3 cup, table-spoons, ¼ cup)
- ☐ Bowls for the ingredients
- ☐ Honey or cinnamon graham cereal
- ☐ Miniature marshmallows
- ☐ Candy coated chocolate can-dies
- ☐ Raisins
- ☐ Small pad of sticky notes
- ☐ Plain paper
- ☐ A marker

**TO DO:**
- ☐ Print the first letter of each word in Matthew 7:11 on a separate sheet of paper, using the version your group is memorizing.
- ☐ Place the various snack items around the room with the ap-propriate serving utensil.

➤ Explain to the kids that during this meeting they will have a special snack that everyone helps prepare. Note for kids that one or two kids will be at each station for the ingredients of the snack and will put in each bag the amount needed and that bags will be passed from station to station.

➤ Place one to two kids at each of these stations:
Station 1) Open the snack bags.
Station 2) Add 1/3 cup cereal.
Station 3) Add ¼ cup of marshmallows.
Station 4) Add two tablespoons of candies.
Station 5) Add one spoon of raisins.

➤ Be sure kids clean their hands before beginning. Guide kids to assemble the snacks in the bags. When all the bags are finished, call for a volunteer to pray, thanking God for the food and the fun they have had at the meeting. Distribute the bags and let kids eat as you continue the meeting.

➤ Review this meeting's Bible story by asking the review questions for this meeting. Ask kids to start naming ways to help others. Explain that you will attach a sticky note to the door frame for each way to help others they name.

Do not take time to write the answer. Just stick the note on the door frame. After a few minutes, call attention to the huge number of ways kids know to help others. Challenge them this week to grow closer to God as they serve others in the ways Jesus did.

- When most kids have finished eating, lead the group to review Matthew 7:11. Allow the kids to place the letter papers you prepared on the floor spaced at least a foot apart from each other.
- Point out that the letters represent the first letters of each word in the verse. Instruct the kids to take turns jumping from letter to letter representing the words of the verse as other kids repeat the verse aloud. Be sure the group repeats the verse slowly enough that the kid can decide which letter, find it, and then jump to it before another word is added. Praise kids for learning this Bible verse.
- Remind kids to complete this week's daily queries in the Younger or Older Kids Activity Book.

# The Quest & Promise

## GOD WILL GO WITH US TO THE END

*Through this study children can...*

**KNOW**
that the Bible is their life-long guide for growing closer to God.

**DISCOVER**
ways to use the Bible in their quests.

**REALIZE**
that obeying God's Word helps them live lives of peace.

*Key Verse:*
Review Matthew 7:7-11

# EMBARK

**YOU WILL NEED:**
- ☐ "Flashlight and Mirrors Target" (Item 29)
- ☐ Flashlight for each team
- ☐ Mirror for each team
- ☐ Masking tape

**TO DO:**
- ☐ Make a tape line on the floor to indicate where kids with flashlights should stand.
- ☐ Post a target for each team, about six feet from the tape line.

**TEACHING TIP**
Another option is to play the game without the mirrors, but time the kids as they run the relay and challenge them to run it again faster.

## SHINE THE TARGET

- Form teams. Give one person on each team a flashlight. Point out each team's target and remark that the player who holds the flashlight must simply shine the light onto the target. Then add that the player must, however, bounce the light off a mirror and onto the target!
- Give a mirror to one player on each team. That player will hold the mirror as the kid with the flashlight directs.
- At your signal, the first player will direct the one holding the mirror by telling him where to stand. The first player then bounces the light from the mirror onto the target.
- After a player shines the light on the target by way of the mirror, he passes the flashlight to the team player behind him and moves to be the holder of the mirror. The previous holder moves to the end of his team's line. The first team with all players completing the task is the winner.
- Note for kids that campers often use flashlights, lanterns, or campfires to give them light during their adventures. Mention that in Bible times, people used oil lamps or simple lanterns to give light as needed. Urge kids to listen during the meeting for times lights or lamps are mentioned.

# EXPLORE

**YOU WILL NEED:**

- ☐ The memory verse posters used in previous meetings (Items 7, 8, 16, 22, and 24)
- ☐ Flashlight
- ☐ Paper plates
- ☐ Scissors
- ☐ Tape
- ☐ Marker
- ☐ (Section #3) "Names for Jesus" (Item 32)
- ☐ (Section #4) "Psalm 119 References" (Item 30)
- ☐ (Section #4) "Lamp and Light Reminders" (Item 31)

**TO DO:**

- ☐ (Section #1) Cut each poster into two or three phrases. Tape each phrase to a different paper plate.

### 1. INTRODUCE THE QUEST

- ➤ Read Psalm 119:105 aloud for kids. Instruct them to hold their Bibles to represent the phrase Your Word. They can hold their Bibles out like camping lanterns to remind them of the word lamp and then hold the Bible like a flashlight to represent light in the verse. Kids can use their own suggestions for feet and path. Repeat this verse along with its actions several times.
- ➤ Remind kids that God's Word is filled with promises to us. The Bible is our life-long guide for growing closer to God.

### 2. TELL THE BIBLE STORY

- ➤ Explain that today's Bible story is about King David listening and obeying God. Direct the kids to locate Deuteronomy 17:14 in their Bibles. Read the verse aloud. Point out that God knew the Israelites would one day want a king, and He told them what a king should do to be a good king.
- ➤ Call on a volunteer to read Deuteronomy 17:18-19. Explain that God commanded Israel's kings to write and read God's laws — the first 5 books of the Bible, Genesis-Deuteronomy. Ask, "How would you feel about writing everything contained in those five Bible books?" Continue by asking how long

the king was to read these Scriptures (all his life) and why the king was to read and write the law (to learn to fear and obey God).

➤ Open your Bible to 1 Samuel 16-17. Explain that the Bible story is about God choosing David to be king of Israel and reminding David and all of Israel that He is always with His people. Even as a boy, God was preparing King David for the good plans He had in store for David. Encourage the kids to remember that fact as they listen to you tell the Bible story.

### DAVID WAS ANOINTED AND FOUGHT GOLIATH
### 1 SAMUEL 16–17

*Saul was not going to be king of Israel anymore. He had disobeyed God. Israel needed a new king, a better king. God told Samuel to visit a man in Bethlehem named Jesse. Jesse had eight sons, and one of them would be Israel's king.*

*Samuel did what God told him to do. He went to Bethlehem to meet with Jesse and his sons. Jesse's oldest son, Eliab, was tall and handsome.*

*"This must be the one God chose to be king," Samuel thought.*

*"Samuel, he's not the one," God said. "Do not pay attention to what he looks like. You look at what you can see on the outside, but I see the heart."*

*One by one, Jesse's sons approached Samuel, but God had not chosen any of them.*

*"Do you have any more sons?" Samuel asked.*

*"Yes," Jesse said. "My youngest son, David, is in the field taking care of the sheep." Jesse sent for David. When David arrived, God told Samuel, "He's the one!"*

*Samuel poured oil on David's head and the Spirit of the Lord was with David. Then Samuel went back home.*

*The Spirit of the Lord was not with Saul anymore. In fact, Saul was bothered by an evil spirit. Saul's servants suggested Saul find someone who could play the harp. Hearing beautiful music might make Saul feel better when the evil spirit bothered him. One of Saul's officials knew just the person to play the harp—David, son of Jesse. David came to Saul and whenever Saul felt troubled, David played his harp and Saul felt better.*

*At this time, Israel's enemies, the Philistines, got ready for war. They were going to attack a town in Judah. King Saul got his army ready to fight. The Israelites camped on one hill while the Philistines camped on another. There was a valley between them.*

*The Philistines had a great warrior named Goliath. At 9 feet 9 inches tall, Goliath was their hero. Goliath shouted at the Israelites, "Why are you lined up, ready for battle? Send me your best man, and we'll fight one-on-one." But none of the Israelites wanted to fight Goliath. They were afraid of him.*

*Jesse's three oldest sons were part of the Israelite army camped on a hill. Jesse sent David to check on his brothers and to give them something to eat. David saw Goliath and watched the Israelites run away in fear. David heard that Saul had offered a great reward to the man who killed Goliath, and David volunteered to fight.*

*"You don't stand a chance against Goliath," Saul argued.*

*"I have killed wild animals," David explained. "God will keep me safe."*

*Saul allowed David to fight Goliath. He offered his armor to David, but David could hardly move. He took off the armor and chose five smooth stones from a nearby stream. David was armed only with the stones and a slingshot.*

*Goliath saw David and made fun of him because he was just a boy.*

*"You come to fight with a spear and sword," David replied, "but I come to fight in the name of God! You have insulted Him, and God always wins His battles!"*

*David ran toward Goliath. He slung a rock at Goliath, and the rock hit Goliath in the forehead. Goliath fell face down, and David killed him without even having a sword.*

### 3. MAKE THE CHRIST CONNECTION

- ➤ Remind kids that the Israelites were up against their toughest enemies, the Philistines. They didn't stand a chance against Goliath, the mighty Philistine warrior. God gave David power to defeat Goliath. David reminds us of Jesus, who came to save us from our greatest enemies: sin and death. Jesus, the ultimate hero, gives us salvation and eternal life.
- ➤ Challenge kids to remember that all Scripture points to Jesus. Note that although David did not know the Savior's name, he did know God promised to send the Savior.

- Mention that Jesus has many names. Form four groups. Give each group a set of letters. Instruct the groups to unscramble their letters to find other names used for Jesus in the Bible.
- Stress that both the Old and New Testaments lead people to Jesus as Savior.

### 4. STUDY THE BIBLE

- Point out that David first learned the law, then learned to obey it. Mention that David grew to love God's commands and that he wrote many psalms about his joy in learning about God from Scripture.
- Distribute the "Psalm 119 References." Direct the whole group to locate Psalm 119. Emphasize that David wrote many psalms, but that Psalms 119 is filled with verses about his love of God's Word.
- Call on kids with reference cards to read their verses from Psalm 119. Point out phrases such as *Your Word, precepts, statutes, promise, commandments, decrees, instruction*, and others that refer to the Scriptures.
- Direct kids' attention to Psalm 119:105 again. Call on two or three kids to read the verse aloud, using various Bible translations if possible.
- Ask what lamps do to help people. (*Help them see what they can't see in the dark*) Explain that David meant God's Word helps people know what God wants them to know and do. God's Word guides and teaches people. God's Word promises that God will go with believers to the end of their quest.

Show one at a time the "Lamp and Light Reminders" as you explain how following them can help them grow closer to God throughout their lives.

**1. Hold onto your lamp, God's Word.**

- God's Word is your lamp for knowing how God wants you to act. When you read your Bible every day and work to learn what is in the Bible, you are holding onto your lamp.

**2. Keep oil in your lamp.**

- Keep the Holy Spirit involved in your reading of Scripture by asking His help in understanding what you read.

**3. Keep the wicks trimmed by reading God's Word every day.**

- The wicks must be trimmed on oil lamps every day they are burned. A person needs to read God's Word every day.

**4. Trust God even when you can't see what He is doing.**

➤ God often reveals things to people through His Word, but even if He does not, you can trust Him to do what is right.

**5. Watch for things God does.**

➤ When you look for what God is doing, you will see wondrous works.

## 5. FOCUS ON THE MEMORY VERSE

➤ Place the plates containing words of Matthew 7:7 on the floor, printed side up. Call on kids to put the plates in order. Lead the group to read the verse aloud together. Continue with the other verses, one at a time, in the same manner.

➤ After all the verses have been reviewed, mix all the plates on the floor in scrambled order. Give a flashlight to one child and let him shine the light on the words in the correct order while kids repeat the verse. Repeat the process with each kid who wants a turn.

➤ Remind the kids that God wants them to ask, seek, and knock during their entire lives and that He will guide them in that quest.

## 6. PRAY

➤ Call for kids to tell prayer requests they have. Print each request on a different paper plate. Then ask what groups of people need their prayers. Expect answers such as hungry, sad, lonely, or sick people. Print each group name on a paper plate. Add the additional plate you prepared.

➤ Explain that in flashlight prayers, one person shines the light on a plate and waits as kids pray silently for the request or group printed on the plate. After a few moments of silence, the kid with the light will pass it to the next person and then turn over the plate he highlighted. The next kid chooses any plate he wants and shines the light on it. Continue in this way until all the plates have been turned over. Add *amen* to the prayer.

# ENGAGE

➤ Transition kids into small groups, dividing them into an older group and younger group. Distribute Activity Books and pencils.

➤ Complete Activity Book pages 38 and 39 to reinforce learning and to go deeper.

## ENGAGE ACTIVITY 1: MAKE STADIUM CUSHIONS WITH A SECRET

**YOU WILL NEED:**

- ☐ Newspapers
- ☐ A vinyl tablecloth or opaque shower curtain for every 6 to 8 kids (to be cut up)
- ☐ Duct tape
- ☐ Scissors

**TO DO:**

- ☐ Cut the tablecloth into 13-by-17-inch rectangles, two per kid.

➤ Remind kids that during Group Time they discovered that God wants people to read His Word regularly. Ask, "What benefits might a person gain from reading the Bible?" Explain that reading the Bible might at first seem like a chore because some words are difficult to understand. Note for kids that as God helps the reader understand the message of the Bible, reading it becomes something to look forward to rather than being a chore.

➤ Ask, "What might be hardest about getting into the habit of reading the Bible every day?" Give tips as needed, such as: Try to read it at the same time each day; put the Bible in a place where you see it often; or read it with your family.

➤ Question the kids about whether they have seen people bring cushions to sporting events or picnics. Remark that seats are often decorated with team symbols. Suggest kids make their own stadium cushions that will remind them to put reading God's Word first in their lives. Point out that they can use the cushions at picnics, sporting events, or other places where they need a seat.

➤ Lead the kids to make the cushions.

➤ Stack newspapers to make rectangles about 11-by-15-inches. (Don't cut the papers. Just fold them to the size.) The stack should be ½ to 1-inch thick.

➤ Tape the edges of the stack together with duct tape.

➤ Distribute the plastic rectangles you cut, two per person. Stack the rectangles with wrong sides together. Tape the rectangles together on two long sides and one short side. (Leave one short side open.)

➤ Slide the newspaper stack into the plastic envelope and tape it shut.

➤ Explain to kids that they can now add the "secret" to their cushions. Kids will use duct tape to print #1 on one side of their cushions. Point out that other people will think they are cheering their team on but the #1 is really to remind the kids that reading their Bibles each day should be their #1 thing to do.

➤ Invite the kids to sit in a circle on the floor, using their cushions. Ask: "What are some things the Bible teaches people to do? How does the Bible tell us to treat God?"

- Ask how old kids can be when they quit reading their Bibles. (Never!) Stress the importance of reading the Bible, learning from it, and doing what God has said in it. Emphasize that God will continue teaching them from the Bible during their entire lives. He has promised it and He will do it.
- Lead the group in prayer, asking God to help kids learn how to have a closer relationship with Him as they read and study the Bible.

### ENGAGE ACTIVITY 2: MAKE A PLAN FOR MEMORIZING BIBLE VERSES

**YOU WILL NEED:**

- ☐ "Memorizing Bible Verses" (Item 33)
- ☐ Index cards (about 10 per kid)
- ☐ Pencils or pens
- ☐ Large sheet of paper
- ☐ Light-weight cardboard or heavy paper (about 5-by-7-inches)
- ☐ Scissors
- ☐ Tape

**TO DO:**

- ☐ Print each of the following Bible references on the sheet of paper: 1 Corinthians 16:8; Psalm 13:10; Psalm 119:105; Ephesians 6:14, Ephesians 6:15, Ephesians 6:16, Ephesians 6:17, Ephesians 6:18; 2 Timothy 3:16, James 1:22.
- ☐ Display the poster for the kids.

- Remind kids that when they read God's Word, God's Holy Spirit teaches them. Memorizing verses from the Bible is important because memorization means God can bring it to a person's mind at any time and in any situation. Tell kids that former prisoners of war often tell about recalling memorized Bible verses with other prisoners and how those Bible verses helped them keep their hope.
- Suggest that kids make an easel to hold cards with Bible verses printed on them and one card with helpful memorization hints. Recommend they keep the easel and its cards where they will be reminded to memorize Bible verses.
- Give each kid about 10 index cards. Show the poster you made. Guide the kids to locate one of the Bible references from the poster and to read it in the Bible. The kid may choose whether to print that verse on an index card or not. Suggest that kids make about 8 to 10 Bible verse cards.
- When kids have completed their cards, guide them to cut out and trace onto heavy paper or light-weight cardboard the pattern for the easel. The pattern is to be placed with the long edge on a fold. Kids cut out their easels and open them slightly so they stand on a table.
- Distribute extra index cards so kids can tape "Tips for Memorizing Bible Verses" onto a card. Kids place their cards on the easel with the tips card at the front.

- Explain that a kid can read the suggestions for memorizing verses and then place that card on the table in front of the easel. The kid then uses those tips to help memorize the verse that is showing at the front of the easel. When the kid has finished, he places the Bible reference card at the back of the cards and places the tips card at the front. Point out that kids can review verses they learned earlier or make new cards to add to their stacks.
- Pray with the kids, asking God to help them learn His Word and how it can help them grow closer to God.

# EXAMINE

**YOU WILL NEED:**

- [ ] Umbrella
- [ ] Masking tape
- [ ] Four small balls (such as ping-pong balls, golf balls, or tennis balls)

**TEACHING TIP**

To play using only one ball, direct kids to form one long line. Kids take turns bouncing the ball. The group works together to accumulate as many points as they can in the time allowed.

- Form a circle of all kids and leaders. Remind the kids that God's Word is a lamp and light that shows them how to live as God wants them to live. Lead the group to repeat Psalm 119:105 using the actions they practiced earlier.
- Instruct kids to hold Bibles. Point out that God will reveal to them many things they do not yet know if they spend time reading and studying it. Pray together, asking God to help each person in the group to want to spend time reading the Bible and to help each one understand what she reads.
- Remark that continuing to ask questions of God is important for one's whole life. Stress that this helps people grow closer to God, which is the most amazing quest anyone can undertake.
- Explain that sometimes real-life adventures involve rain. Place an umbrella upside down at one end of the room. Direct two kids to make a tape box around the umbrella about 5 square feet or so. Let kids choose on which side of the square they want to stand. Give a ball to one player on each side. Call a number between 1 and 3. The player with the ball tries to toss the ball in such

a way that it bounces that number before landing in the umbrella. If a player gets the ball in the umbrella in the correct number of bounces, he tells a fact about King David moving the ark to Jerusalem to earn his team a point. Note that all teams may earn a point on each question if they all have the correct number of bounces. If the leader calls "Rain Storm," any number of bounces is allowed. Teams whose balls land in the umbrella all get a point if they name a fact.

- After several rounds, lead kids to play the game naming facts about other Bible stories or verses they have learned during The Quest. Keep the game going until all kids have been picked up.
- As kids leave, remind them to complete this week's daily queries.